Porthleven, Past And Present: Scenes From The History Of A Cornish Fishing Village

Martin Veall, John Howard Harris

Nabu Public Domain Reprints:

You are holding a reproduction of an original work published before 1923 that is in the public domain in the United States of America, and possibly other countries. You may freely copy and distribute this work as no entity (individual or corporate) has a copyright on the body of the work. This book may contain prior copyright references, and library stamps (as most of these works were scanned from library copies). These have been scanned and retained as part of the historical artifact.

This book may have occasional imperfections such as missing or blurred pages, poor pictures, errant marks, etc. that were either part of the original artifact, or were introduced by the scanning process. We believe this work is culturally important, and despite the imperfections, have elected to bring it back into print as part of our continuing commitment to the preservation of printed works worldwide. We appreciate your understanding of the imperfections in the preservation process, and hope you enjoy this valuable book.

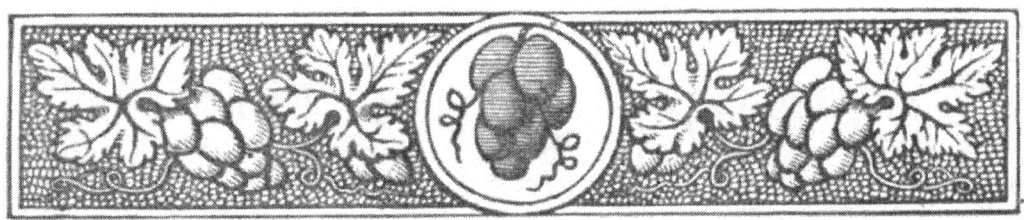

EDITORIAL NOTE.

THE idea of publishing this little volume belongs to Mr. Martin Veall, Porthleven, who furnished material for the purpose. To suit the following pages his MSS. have been supplemented by the addition of important facts. I am under considerable obligation to Captain Rogers, R.A., Penrose, for the loan of valuable private papers; to Mr. John Rowe, Porthleven, for practical suggestions and legal documents; and to Mr. Louis C. Read, Superintendent of H.M. Customs, and Receiver of Wreck, Penzance, to whose courtesy I am indebted for information of a highly entertaining character. Thanks are due to many others for the cheerful assistance they have rendered. The illustrations are the gift of an amateur. In conclusion, it may be stated that there is ample and interesting matter at my disposal to

CONTENTS.

CHAP.		PAGE
I.	EARLY HISTORY	9
II.	BYGONE SCENES AND CHARACTERS	15
III.	SMUGGLING—THE OLD CUSTOM HOUSE	25
IV.	WRECKS AND DISASTERS AT SEA	34
V.	THE HARBOUR	54
VI.	GROWTH OF METHODISM	65
VII.	PORTHLEVEN PRESENT	80

CHAPTER I.

EARLY HISTORY.

PORTHLEAVEN, or Port Levan Cove, was on the eastern side of Mount's Bay, Cornwall. Inland ran a winding valley, at the bottom of which a little river pursued its seaward course. The mouth of this valley was divided from the sea by a sand or gravel bank, into which sandbar the stream referred to ran. Over this embankment the waves flowed during stormy weather; and thus were formed a miniature Loe Bar and Loe Pool, in imitation of the larger one so well known, about a mile further east. In this pond—*The Owan*—the boys were accustomed to sail their toy boats, and watch with delight the movements of one which was cutter-rigged, and carried a tinkling bell; while some adventurous lads occasionally attempted its navigation in the family

blossom in the spring and summer. These yellow clusters concealed many a bird's nest from observation, but failed to secure them from the quest of juveniles who made the *Reens* their resort, searching for blackberries and bluebells, or digging ground-nuts—*keggas* they termed them. The stream, not far from the Owan, was crossed by a stone bridge, formed by placing a slab of rock on two upright supports. Further up was a marsh or moor that produced an abundant crop of rushes, and over which in winter might have been heard the heron's cry or the shrill whistle of the plover.

Standing on the bridge, and looking landward, a few thatched cottages could have been descried on the left, or Breage side, and on the right, or Sithney side. The stream divided the two parishes. The dwellings were of humble pretensions, but were picturesque in their quaintness. The majority were built with ends seaward, as security against the winter storm. A little stone-paved court, surrounded by a low wall, and entered by a door, led to the cottage threshold, and a glance would have revealed the cleanliness of the interior. On the "lime-ash" floors, well sprinkled with fine sand, stood the

lamp, must be reckoned. The latter consisted of an earthenware or metal stand, like an ordinary candlestick, from which rose a shaft or stem, which supported the vessel containing the train-oil. The wick floated in the liquid, and its end rested in a lip or beak made in the top vessel. In the west of Cornwall this kind of lamp was the ordinary source of illumination, and the train-oil seller, with pitcher and measure, was a regular visitor at many homesteads.

In the wide chimney corners burned the peat fires, under the ashes of which choice meals were prepared, whose flavour would delight an epicure, and up which roared the flames of great wood-fires, while the stars peeped down on the ruddy cheeks of the cottagers.

In rear of the houses was a little cultivated land, whence the subsistence of the few families was partly derived. Some, on the Sithney side, had gardens which sloped down to the valley bottom. Combined with agricultural employment was a little fishing in boats of a small size. When an opportunity offered smuggling was eagerly followed, and, perhaps, like

character. An examination of the sand and pebbles revealed their silicious or flinty nature, and this would lead the ingenious observer to conclude that flint was obtainable from the cliffs adjacent. An investigation, however, would satisfy one that such could not be found. Whence came this belt of shifting sand and shingle? On the western side, too, of the cove, was a huge detached granitic mass, locally designated the "Giant's Quoit"; but no granite is to be discovered in the cliff side adjoining. Whence came it? Tradition speaks of the arrival of the beach in *one* night during a severe storm. It has also been suggested that both boulder and pebbles were brought by disembodied spirits—notably the great Tregeagle—as acts of penance. Their sacks and aprons must have been in frequent requisition to accomplish so much! But the theory of the scientist is that it is the result of glacial action in the bygone ages. Be this as it may, the western commencement of this beach, near Porthleven Cove, was backed by greensward. The wheel of a *grist*

in the old mill, by having a certain measure retained as payment, we will not attempt to surmise; or whether the man of flour occasionally "tulled the corn" *twice* we cannot tell: the old wheel and the old mill-house have long since disappeared, but traces of their former position remain. It was named the *Torleven Mill*, Torleven being a portion of old Porthleven. Romance has fashioned a legend of the "Miller's Daughter," and refers the story to the privateering times of the old French wars; but the facts are wanting to fill in the outline of what might have proved a fascinating narrative.

Where bare rocks are now to be seen, near the site of the mill was a pleasant little extent of green turf, on which was constructed a summer-house. It is difficult at the present time to associate verdure with the barren rocks washed by the sea and the spray. Yet here stood a little cot, used as a summer resort by some local ladies—the late Lady Bassett, of Tehidy, and the members of the family of the late John Rogers, Esq., of Penrose. This sea-side dwelling was then, and long afterwards, known as the *Mew*. It must have been used only during the warm weather. In the winter its eaves might have

of summer-house and sward has long since passed away; nothing now remains but rock, pools, and sand.

A little eastward of the Mew stood a capstan, of great use to the fishermen. By its aid the boats were drawn up on the beach, out of the reach of the surf. When the weather was stormy, the capstan was manned by willing helpers, and the boat drawn slowly and skilfully beyond the action of the billows. Sometimes it was a dangerous undertaking, and unless manœuvred with alacrity and steadiness, the boat was caught by the falling wave and freed of nets and gear, and, perhaps, afterwards tossed battered on the beach.

Such was Porthleven a century or more ago. The old cottages are gone, but that occupied by Mr. Peter Kitchen seems to be the oldest now remaining, and is a model of quaintness and cleanliness. What the hamlet was like previously we will leave to the imagination of the reader, suggesting, however, that the remains of roots, branches, and nuts in a blackened state in the valley mud and under the sandbar at its mouth, as well as the occurrence of timber of large size, red inside, in the same locality, point to the distant days when Methleigh Valley, like

CHAPTER II.

BYGONE SCENES AND CHARACTERS.

IN a rickety armchair sat Dame James, the village schoolmistress. She usually selected the corner of the little room wherein to establish her throne. Armed with a willow wand of surprising length, she was the personification of Law and Order. Her attire would scarcely fulfil the requirements of a modern high-school governess, being of a style long since departed, yet common enough in the days of our grandparents. On her head was a white muslin cap with a *jenny-quick'd* border, as it was then termed, to which kind of border the old ladies were very partial. Her arms and body were encased in a close-fitting *bedgown*, a dress that showed to advantage, or otherwise,

was a secondary consideration. The sides of a low bedstead supplied seats, for be it known that the schoolroom was also bedroom. Enthroned in the corner, Dame James called the children to her side, where they read or spelled aloud from a well-worn primer. During the reading or spelling sundry orders were given to certain of the scholars, the delivery of which must have interfered with the scholastic routine. One would be commanded—" Go for a pennard (pennyworth) of snuff." Perhaps, by way of change, the order might have been—" Get a hounce of tay for me"; while another pupil would receive the intimation—" Blaw the fire." The effect of the instruction must have been seriously impaired by the following method :—In the midst of a child's spelling lesson, Master Will, one of the dame's disciples, would have the peremptory direction—" Taake the waater-pot, Will, and go down to Cliff Will (well) for a turn of waater to put in the kittle." Then turning her attention once more to the business of instruction she would say—" Now, thee go on with thy lesson. N-a-u-g-h-t. Well! what es that? Don't knaw! Thee do'sn't knaw,

While these matters were in progress the school-bell would be rung. The bell deserves a record, as it would well merit a sketch in an antiquarian's note-book. The *bell* was nothing more or less than an old iron kettle, which was struck by a rusty bolt attached to a string. When "missus" wanted her tea the school-bell would be rung by order, perhaps a quarter of an hour previous to the ordinary time of dismissal—an arrangement satisfactory to the children.

From day to Sunday school description is an easy transition. Perhaps a reference to the Sabbath school weekly march to the neighbouring parish church of Sithney, about three miles distant, will be of interest. It is a sunlit Sunday morning in 1815. The scholars have donned their best attire. Drawn up in line in front of the chapel they present a singular appearance. The girls are looking very attractive in their cottage bonnets, which are carefully tied under the chin with a band of plain green ribbon. The boys are clad in their usual Sunday clothes. Preceded by the girls (the seniors of the school), the boys form into couples, and set off for their long walk. The scholars are accompanied by

neck by a piece of green ribbon. Each label, of the size of a small dessert plate, is painted green, and on this ground, in white letters, about an inch long, is painted the rank or office each holds: *e.g.*, Superintendent, Treasurer, Secretary, Bible-teacher, Monitor, etc. Through flower-scented lanes, and meadows clover-blossomed, the little procession moves steadily on, with hearts, let us hope, full of thankfulness to the Great Giver. While they are wending their way as Christian soldiers, their countrymen in distant Belgium on this very Sabbath morn must be commencing the memorable battle of Waterloo. In due time the bonneted maidens and their labelled protectors arrive at Sithney church, an hour before the commencement of the service. Here they practise the chants and hymns preparatory to Morning Prayer. This morning march was repeated every Sunday morning, but its observance has long since disappeared.

It is very probable that certain of the scholars referred to in the last paragraph resided in the row of houses known as Buenos Ayres. The general reader will wonder at the name of a South American city figuring so prominently in a Cornish fishing

"Manor and Liberty of Winnianton: Parish of Gunwallo.

Lost—part of the contents of a trunk, belonging to a lady: viz., a diamond ring; two chain necklaces; dollars; and other money. Also a large quantity of linen. Whoever will bring the above to Penrose shall be handsomely rewarded; and should any of the articles be offered for sale to silversmiths or others, they are desired to stop the parties and carry them before the magistrate.

"Execrations on the plunderers of the widow and the orphan are in the mouths of all I meet. The magistrates are determined to do their duty: let the people do the same, and the disgrace of the country will be done away."

A week previous to the publication of this proclamation, a transport—the *James and Rebecca*, No. 42, Robert Rochester, master—became a total wreck under the neighbouring Hal-zephron Cliff. On board were 200 of the 9th Regiment of Dragoons (dismounted), in addition to their officers, officers wives, and the vessel's crew. The transport was

November 6th, the *James and Rebecca* came ashore, at ten o'clock, during a terrific storm.

About eleven o'clock next day she went to pieces, and the scene is described as most heart-rending. Sailors and soldiers lay drowned on the beach. Thirty men met with a watery grave; the women, eight in number, were saved. The whole of the dead shared *one* common tomb on the cliffs. A certain Edward Pascoe jumped down into the huge pit, arranged the bodies, and scrambled out. Standing on the edge of the grave this Cornish farm labourer read from the Prayer-Book, to the best of his ability, the beautiful words of the impressive Burial Service. This was previous to the passing of the Davies-Gilbert Act, which we intend to refer to again in another chapter.

It is affirmed that all might have been easily landed, but they were reluctant to leave the transport, which contained "piles of plunder." The issue of the notice, relative to the valuable trunk, which must, in all probability, have been the possession of an officer's wife, and the fact that a considerable

stormy day there came the Great Overflowing. The boats in the cove were cast by the waves "up in the moors," and were there left amid the mud and rushes of the marsh. The wharves, in course of erection, were considerably damaged. Near the cottages floated drowned pigs and poultry, while the angry waves entered the kitchens and lower apartments, undermining the walls. The floors were covered with sand and gravel, in which the following day the old folks were seen *riddlin'* for buried pans and crockeryware. Piece by piece the old houses disappeared, until scarcely one stone remains upon another.

Not far from this bygone street lived one of the most influential old gentlemen of Old Porthleven. He merits a notice here. His means were in excess of the majority of his neighbours, by whom he was considered of more than ordinary importance; consequently his opinion was valued, and his advice generally followed. He must have associated with persons of breeding and distinction somewhere, judging from the courtly air of his deportment, and from his usual outfit. If a stranger

ance, and this conjecture would have been heightened by a glance at his capacious coat. The latter had large sleeves and expansive cuffs, while the shining buttons ornamenting the garment were as large as five-shilling-pieces. On his feet were low shoes, fastened by brightly polished silver buckles, while his knee-breeches had buckles of the same metal. Altogether he seemed a personage of distinction. Was he a French count in disguise? No; he was a native production, and possessed an importance beyond the shores of Mount's Bay. He was summoned to London to give evidence before a commission concerning the need of a harbour for his native hamlet. With praiseworthy diligence he prepared for the investigation by attending to his garments and seeing to the general state of his wardrobe. The buckles were brightened; the buttons looked like mirrors; and his *wide-awake* hat seemed more dignified. His red waistcoat needed attention from skilful fingers, as there was a rent of some sort on one side. This was duly patched with a piece of *new* material, which stood out prominently from its somewhat faded surroundings. In due time London, with all its mysteries, was reached, and our nautical-

subject for their sarcasm. After he had been in the metropolis a day or two, his surprise and mortification can be imagined when he saw his own figure and habiliments caricatured in the print shops! Yes; there was his likeness in many a window,—broad brim, wide-sleeved coat, and the unfortunate red patched waistcoat, all complete,—and, under the portrait of one so popular at home, the inscription—A CORNISH FISHERMAN!!

Very eccentric was the hallucination of one of our old inhabitants. Uncle R—— was haunted with the belief that he had *glass legs!* From morn till eve the thought of his fragile limbs was ever harassing his mind, and making life burdensome. He was afraid to move lest they should crack off like a nutshell. If any one attempted to touch him he shrank back in terror for the safety of his brittle legs. He had not always thus been worried. Many is the time Uncle R—— drew harmonious sounds from the depths of his *bass viol*, for be it understood he was a skilful wielder of the bow; and many a passer-by received the enticing invitation, "Comest thee in here, and I'll play 'Leverpool' for thee!" If Uncle R—— had lived in Porthleven some years

CHAPTER III.

SMUGGLING—THE OLD CUSTOM HOUSE.

DURING the early part of the eighteenth century a Government building was erected at Porthleven, and an official was appointed for the *preventing*, as far as possible, of smuggling. The old building remains, in a somewhat ruinous condition, and is still called the old Custom House.

It was no unusual occurrence in those days to see parties of from ten to twenty men, on horseback, riding through Porthleven, with kegs of brandy or gin slung across the horses' backs. Darkness was not always desired for such nefarious practices, as they frequently accosted the preventive officer in the daytime, while they jeeringly rode by with the

a law-breaker. Fines, or imprisonment in His Britannic Majesty's navy, were the usual penalties of the captured.

Smuggling during the last century, to quote the words of a modern writer, "was considered a *virtue*. The revenue officers were esteemed public enemies." Possessing such *virtuous spirit*, what wonder is it that many of our ancestors engaged in the "smuggling service"?

The eastern coast of Mount's Bay presented many natural facilities for carrying on contraband operations, and many is the *tub* of Hollands gin or Cognac that has been submerged in its coves or secreted in its caves. There were few village families at that date lacking representatives in the smuggling "interest." To make a run to Nantes for a few kegs of Cognac (in smuggler phraseology "Cousin Jacky"), and to land their cargo successfully, formed no extraordinary event. The *honest* folk in the construction of their dwellings provided for the concealment of the "spirits." They were laid to rest in the false backs and bottoms of cupboards, or lodged in hidden shafts at the foot of the stairs. Some houses contained small chambers in the thickness

their "cousin" under the pile of sand or wood that usually stood in the "'ood" (wood) corner of the kitchens. Examples of some of these secret store-places still remain in Porthleven. A recent discovery of such a hiding-place was lately brought under our notice. At a farmhouse, not far from Porthleven, an ordinary hearthstone seems fixed in the flooring near the fireplace. Knocking on this stone no hollow sound is given out, as might be the case if an open space were beneath. But remove the stone, and then read the cunning of the designer's mind. A thick layer of earth conceals a *second* slab of rock. The latter being lifted, a flight of steps is observed, leading to an underground apartment, sufficiently large to accommodate half-a-dozen "jolly good fellows."

The means devised to check this breach of Imperial legislation were inadequate. To prevent smuggling being carried on over a coast a dozen miles in length, the preventive force at one period consisted of an officer and crew, who were stationed at Porthleven. Their official duties were supple-

Amusing stories are on record of the preventive men being themselves *prevented*, sometimes by invitation to partake of "Coz Jack," or, as once happened, by being taken *vi et armis* and deposited in a ditch while the captors proceeded to discharge a cargo. The following incident will show to what uncanny usage the officers of the Crown were subjected in the good old days. It was narrated to a friend by a participator in the "run" described.

A cargo of goods was being landed on a certain beach when two *colours' men* (officers) were seen approaching. Soon they were in the midst of the smugglers, who suddenly seized the officers, and bound them hand and foot. The unhappy preventive men were placed in their helpless condition just *above high-water mark*, where they were left with the remark, "Dead cocks can't crow!" They begged for mercy, and promised secrecy for freedom. When the business of landing the spirit was complete, the *prevented* men were set at liberty.

Bang! came a knock at the old Custom House

informer, who was ready to disclose the hiding-place of a large quantity of contraband spirits. If the said smuggled liquor were found and secured, he (the informant) was to receive a stated sum of money. A written agreement was signed to that effect.

Upon the departure of this midnight visitor messengers were sent to the neighbouring villages, with instructions to the officers to assemble at a given rendezvous. They were ordered to do so without delay, and to bring the soldiery with them, to assist them in their duty, if required.

Having all assembled at the place appointed, they set out for the spot to which they had been directed—not a great way from Porthleven. Reaching their destination—a certain house—a part entered, while a portion of the men remained outside in case of any emergency arising.

The party who had entered the house, to the no small surprise of the inmates, without further ceremony went directly to a cupboard and took up some loose boards. These formed a false bottom, and beneath was a cave or underground cellar into which the searchers descended. Here they discovered *hundreds* of kegs of smuggled spirits, chiefly

subterranean passage still exists, but the seaward outlet cannot be found, as the rocks have fallen together, or "runn'd in," as miners term it.

Just before this discovery was made, one morning, at early dawn, a smart little clipper brig was seen running out to sea from the coast near the locality of the seizure of goods referred to. There being something suspicious in her appearance, a Revenue cruiser, then in the bay, gave chase. The trim little brig soon distanced her pursuer, and the latter, after firing a shot or two, which fell short, gave up the pursuit. It is a fair conjecture to conclude that the captured brandy had been landed from this vessel which had cleverly made her escape.

About the same period a beautiful green-painted shallop of great length, and lugger-rigged, was met with in the bay by a cruiser. Having a suspicious look about her, she was brought to Porthleven, and detained. She had pretty white sails, and rowed twelve oars. After diligent investigation no evidence was to be obtained of her being employed in smuggling; consequently, after a few days' detention,

floating on the water. The gale subsiding, and a shift of wind having rendered it practicable for boats to go out, two of them, in charge of Sulifan, a pilot, put to sea. After some difficulty they secured the two strings of kegs, numbering more than a hundred, and brought the brandy and gin safely into Porthleven. Here the Custom House officer took possession in the name of the Crown. The men who went out in the boats were handsomely rewarded. It afterwards transpired that the contraband goods were the cargo of the yacht-like shallop we have described.

The smuggled liquor was much in request by the country people living inland. They often set out on horseback for the coast, returning in the evening with one or more little casks strapped to the saddle. The coveted Cognac was secreted under the sand in the "'ood" corner. Here it remained for a little while until bottled. Those engaged in bottling the spirit frequently showed signs of intoxication, arising from the strong fumes of the gin or brandy, while some are said to have been killed in this way. Sometimes a lover of the fire water was seen boring a hole in the keg with a gimlet or other tool, through which aperture the liquid was sucked by means of a quill.

results followed the neglect of stopping the spile-hole, as the following incident will show.

On one occasion a Porthleven resident, finding her supply of smuggled spirits, wherewith her acquaintances were sometimes furnished, decreasing, sent for her "trusty-man," who was no novice at the duty, and said:—

"Matthey, my gin is nearly out."

"Well, missus, what must I do?"

"You must go as soon as you can, Matthey, and get some."

"All right, I'll go to-night; please, missus, for the money!"

Having obtained the funds for his purchase, away went honest Matthew on his errand. He succeeded in obtaining two small kegs of spirits, one of brandy, and one of best Hollands gin. Slinging the kegs pannier-fashion over the horse's back, the "trusty-man" set off homewards, first taking a good drop to help him on the way. He arrived at Porthleven in the early morn, and found his mistress awaiting

"You knaw, Matthey. Be quick!"

Matthew went out, but what must have been his dismay, when he found the kegs—but *empty!*

He had taken a drop at starting, and on his homeward journey met an old acquaintance, and for "auld lang syne" must needs offer him a taste of the grog that hadn't paid any duty. The brandy cask was spiled, and a satisfactory quaff obtained through the spile-hole. Would he not try the beautiful Hollands also? The merits of the latter were tested, and the friends parted. Alas, Matthew! you have forgotten to stop the spile-hole, and long ere you reach Porthleven your brandy and gin will have mingled with the highway dust.

It will be of interest to those acquainted with the old Custom House if we quote from a letter received from the Commissioner of Customs:—"There is no record as to the date at which the Custom House at Porthleven was built, but there is a record showing that rent was paid for officers' residences in the year 1749. The earliest record of an officer at Porthleven is dated 23rd July, 1748, where mention

CHAPTER IV.

WRECKS AND DISASTERS AT SEA

AN account of the shipwrecks that have occurred at or near Porthleven would form a volume of exceeding interest. However, with the space at our disposal, we propose to select a few noteworthy wrecks for description.

November 21*st*, 1738. On November 21st, 1738, the *Vigilantia*, of and for Hamburgh was wrecked westward of Porthleven. The vessel was from Lisbon, and was laden with salt (at that time heavily taxed), tobacco, sugar, and lemons. Of the crew Captain Heinrich and three seamen were drowned; the mate and five sailors were saved. Such was the violence of the waves that the ship was broken to pieces. All the cargo was lost. It is

December 29th, 1738. A month later, the *Naboth's Vineyard*, of Rotterdam, commanded by Tobuen Rich, and homeward bound from Bayonne with a cargo of wine, was driven ashore a little to the eastward. Master and crew reached the shore in safety. The Collector of Customs for the district soon repaired to the scene of the wreck. He was accompanied by soldiers, who received his orders to protect the property washed ashore. Their exertions to rescue portions of the cargo were successful, and several hogsheads of wine were locked up in places of security. After the salvage of the wine from the *Naboth's Vineyard*, a difficulty arose concerning the division of the money, and the owners instructed a local solicitor, Mr. Peter Hill, of Helston (whose monumental tablet is to be seen in Helston Church), to act on their behalf. Three justices of the peace met at Marazion to adjudicate on the case; and on the 14th of March the gentlemen assembled to give their award. After some little dispute the matter was compromised.

December 14th, 1739. During a severe gale a Dutch vessel, the *Lady Lucy*, of Rotterdam, was wrecked

aware of the event. In the absence of the preventive men the ship was plundered, and casks of wine and Cognac were rolled or pulled up rugged cliff paths to hiding-places known only to the initiated. Bags of coffee, too, were transported to cottage cupboards, while Cæsar's name was openly defied. But *next day* the officials made amends for their seeming tardiness. With exceeding diligence they searched the country round, and succeeded in alighting on the concealed brandy casks, which were borne off with all despatch. One worthy neighbouring resident, a clergyman, was somewhat disconcerted to find that the *four* hogsheads in his cellar were rudely carried off on the shoulders of the busy officials! Perhaps he had procured the wine for parochial purposes!

December 3rd, 1748. Three years after the second Stuart rebellion we find the occurrence of a famous(?) Porthleven wreck. From Bordeaux sailed the Dutch ship, *Yonge Alida*, for Amsterdam. On board were 167 tons of wine, which Pear Pearce, the master, trusted his "goot" ship would safely bear to Holland

was carried off by the excited folk. It must have been a bewildering time for the new officer, Sampson, who had been barely six months in the village. He and his assistants were powerless. They dared not interfere. Had they attempted to take away any of the wine kegs from the stalwart Cornishmen, doubtless semi-intoxicated, they would have experienced rough usage. The soldiery, of whom sixty were stationed in West Cornwall to aid the customs' officers, were absent—perhaps called away by the Rebellion of '45. Sampson must have witnessed strange scenes on December 3rd, 1748. Cask after cask disappeared along the country lanes, or was dragged into the thatched cottages. Shouts and boisterous laughter arose on all sides and greeted the hapless officer. The youths and women pulled away the battered wreckage, or pillaged the sea-chests of the unfortunate Hollanders. Drunken carousals in many a house of the country-side followed the shipwreck.

After the excitement connected with the wreck

cask of the *Yonge Alida* wine was concealed in a neighbouring homestead, at Gunwalloe, search was made for it. The hogshead was discovered, seized in the name of the Crown, and the official seal affixed. But a difficulty arose. The wine cask, duly ornamented with the king's mark, had to be removed from the cotter's dwelling, and conveyed to Penzance. The feeling of the people was such that no *plough* could be procured on which the captured "Bordeaux" could be drawn to the Custom House. (By means of a staple the plough was fixed to a thick piece of wood, and so drawn along.) After two days the officers appeared with this novel vehicle to remove the wine over rugged roads to Penzance; but the hogshead had disappeared, and the occupant of the dwelling told his visitors that he had given two guineas for it, and offered to compensate them for their trouble! It will not be wondered at that a petition to the Commissioners was despatched 28th January, 1749, in which letter the collector represented that it would be impossible

off Rochefort. Such were the instructions of Admiral Lord Gardner. By the courtesy of the Admiralty we have been favoured with a copy of a letter sent by Thomas Gill, second lieutenant, from which we quote an extract:—

"The next day (25th) it came on to blow, and continued increasing till the morning of the 28th, when the captain thought proper to bear up for Falmouth. The same day, about 4 o'clock, we made the land to the westward of the Lizard, and in a situation (off the Loe Bar) that compelled us to anchor. At 4 the next morning we parted the best bower, and at 7 the small bower, when the captain directed the ship to be run on shore. She was wrecked this morning (29th) near Port Levan, about two miles from this place (Helston)."

The letter, dated "Helston, 29th December, 1807," is addressed by the lieutenant to the Honourable Wm. Wellesley Pole.

From the shore the ill-fated vessel was seen nearing the beach. The white sea-water streamed from her port-holes as the huge billows dashed against her sides. At length she struck, and notwithstand-

hearts of the spectators. Aid could not be rendered, heroic as many of the shoremen undoubtedly were; certain destruction awaited him who ventured in that thundering surf. One poor sailor was seen suspended from a port-hole, his arm having been jammed there by the shifting of a gun. By-and-by the bone must have cracked, muscles and tendons alone keeping him from dropping. In a short time these, too, yielded, and down he went. The commander, his first lieutenant, and fifty seamen, were drowned, Captain Lydiard's body being afterwards discovered by the Edward Pascoe who figured at the transport wreck. The survivors of the *Anson*, under the direction of the remaining officers, salved portions of the wreckage. A few casks of rum were secured and stored at Porthleven. A sergeant of the local militia being deputed to take charge of a waggon-load of valuables from the bar to Helston, was accosted on his homeward drive by an individual who had matured a scheme for his own benefit. He met the waggon driver, and offered him £50 to be allowed to

shelter at the old public-house, kept by the late Thomas Stodden. On one of the beds upstairs they placed jewellery, watches, and other articles of value, while the floor was littered with clothing, or heaped with heavy materials saved from the wreck. Over these stood a tall soldier on guard with drawn sword in hand, while one of the beams under the bedroom floor was bent with the superincumbent weight. The bent beam may still be seen.

On the cliffs pits were dug in which the drowned seamen were thrown in heaps. There was no attempt at burial service of even simple character; such was the custom. Amongst the folks living on the sea-coast the method pursued on finding a human body washed ashore was to dig a grave for it at the nearest convenient place, usually on the summit of the cliff. Finder to be sexton seemed the rule. But such was the popular indignation with regard to the manner in which the poor fellows of the *Anson* were bundled into their graves, that immediate action was taken. Owing to the representation of the late Mr. Thomas Grylls, who was much struck with the barbarous procedure of burial, an Act of Parliament, locally known as Grylls' Act,

interment in Churchyards or Parochial Burying Grounds in England for such dead bodies as may be cast on shore from the sea in cases of wreck or otherwise." Since 1808, the bodies of persons washed ashore have been laid to rest with Christian rites in the nearest churchyard at the expense of the parish.

Besides the Act of Parliament (called *The Gold-Martial* Act by the old people) there was another important outcome of the *Anson* wreck. Among the witnesses on the Bar or adjoining cliffs was the late Mr. H. Trengrouse, of Helston. He was greatly affected by such destruction of precious life. He was led to consider means whereby such loss might be decreased. To his skill and ingenuity the maritime world is indebted for the noble rocket apparatus—noble in its mission of deliverance. His invention could be used on shore or on shipboard. Experiments were made before official, critical committees with Trengrouse's Rocket, and its efficiency and superiority were conclusively demonstrated. In an old engraving of the *Anson*, published to illustrate the working of the Rocket, is seen how the line

Webb, of Penrose:—"This box formed a portion of the *Anson* frigate, wrecked on the Loe Pool Bar of sand December 28th, 1807. The fir-wood enclosed therein is a portion of the Brazilian barque *Santesta*, wrecked on the sands about a mile east of the Loe Pool Bar, November 1865. The dollar is one of about fourteen tons, wrecked in 1785. It was recovered from the celebrated 'Dollar-Hole,' near Gunwalloe Church Cove, February 1865.

"Found and presented to S. Higgs, Esq., French Consul, etc., at Penzance, by Wm. Webb. . . . Penrose, April 1866."

The frigate was strongly built, as she did not break up until 3 p.m. Sometimes it is stated that 100 were drowned; but we believe many of the crew reached the shore in safety and deserted. This was the confession of one—an old man of Breage, who used to work on the roads. The old folks say they have seen the *Anson's* guns on the sea bottom, and they imagine a part of the vessel is now somewhere in the bay. Be this as it may, no story is

fruit (oranges). She came ashore at Porthleven, a little east of the Institute, in the evening, and held together until the 6th. In spite of the exertions of the officers only 59 casks were secured; these were lodged in the large storehouse (Breage side), then lately built by the Harbour Company.

The people seem to have grown excited at the event of this shipwreck; the old men still speak of scenes which then occurred. The officials were aided by 1 sergeant, 3 corporals, and 12 privates of the Inniskilling Dragoons, then stationed at Pendennis Castle, Falmouth. But, nothing daunted, the country people seized the casks, smashed in the heads, and drank so deeply that some barely escaped death. Others carried off all they could in pails, pans, and buckets, and it is said that so rich was the port wine that some bore it away in *flour bags!* Giving "two hurrahs!" the folks rose against the soldiery, and drove them from the beach. Two accidents happened. A south-countryman (Lizard district), named Gundry, was drowned, while a woman was so frightened at the uproar against the

Falmouth gentleman concerning the custody of the wine. Ultimately a portion of the port was sold at Porthleven to meet expenses, and the amount obtained was £963. The cellars of the principal gentlemen of the neighbourhood became stocked with this choice old wine, and on any special occasion—birth, marriage, or public banquet—healths were drunk and congratulations offered in "old *Resolution*"! Mr. John Kendall, of the Union Bank, Helston, at the time had a good supply of the wine. He liberally and generously used it among his friends and the sick of the town. His son, Mr. E. P. Kendall, of the Bolitho Bank, still has a few bottles of "*Resolution*" in stock.

Rough as our ancestors undoubtedly were, we know that the coves and hamlets of Mount's Bay now contain as brave and bold a body of men as can be produced anywhere. Ready to venture their lives to save their fellows, they are foremost at the shipwreck to rescue storm-tossed seamen. Of their humanity and heroism Porthleven men have frequently given proof, and not a few are the distinctions they have received for spirited conduct.

boat Institution. Through the kindness of the son of the winner (Mr. John Rowe), authenticated by Mr. Charles Dibdin, F.R.G.S., the genial Secretary of the Institution, we are in a position to give a few particulars of the wreck of the brig *Olive*, lost April 1824, under Halzephron Cliffs. The vessel, a collier, bound from Tenby to Littlehampton, carried a crew of seven hands. There was also a female on board, Bridget Williams, the captain's sister. During the night it blew a perfect hurricane, and at daybreak the little brig could be seen beating about in the bay. For a ship to be embayed in Mount's Bay during a south-west gale means—destruction. To the right and left is an almost unbroken coastline, pitiless in its ruggedness, and unprovided with any large harbour of refuge. Porthleven was to windward of the *Olive*, and an anchor being let go, she rode securely for a little time. The cable parted, and she drove before the wind, striking under a precipitous cliff, unequalled for height in the bay. She came ashore near the site of the wreck of the

To the crew death seemed near, as the efforts of the rescuing party appeared vain—wave after wave hurling them back on the shingle. At length a tall young man, no doubt W. Rowe, was noticed to dash into the surf. Around his body a rope was tied, and the men on the vessel saw him making strenuous attempts to reach them. The sea was running very high, and occasionally he was lost sight of, being knocked down and buried in the breakers. But returning to his undertaking again and again, a glad cheer at length proclaimed the success of his venture. By the efforts of this brave Cornish hero, supplemented by the heroic exertions of others equally as daring, *every* life was saved. In a short time not a vestige of the brig could be seen except tangled rigging and floating timber. The captain informed the then Mayor of Helston (H. M. Grylls, Esq., son of T. Grylls, Esq., already mentioned) that the cargo of culm, worth £1,100, was not insured. A subscription for the gallant fishermen was started by the mayor. An application was made by him for a grant from the funds of the Lifeboat Institution, and at their *first* meeting, in July 1824, the sum of £30 was forwarded for distribution among those

leven, the second to John Freeman, of Gunwalloe, in recognition of their brave conduct.

The tourist *en route* to the Lizard from Porthleven would bid adieu to the village at *Gravesend*. The word has a mournful significance. Many a drowned sailor, nameless and coffinless, reposes on the cliffs of our picturesque coast. After the frosts of winter huge masses of rocks, roots, and loose stones fall to the sands, and reveal here and there the whitened bones of shipwrecked mariners. At Gravesend many such vestiges have been seen. It is related by an inhabitant that her mother was startled one morning—about ninety years ago—to see nine bodies laid on the grass awaiting burial in one common grave on the edge of the cliff near the quarry. The registers of some parish churches contain brief records concerning the finding and interment of bodies found on the sea-shore. Invariably brief are such accounts, but eminently pathetic. In the registers of St. Bartholomew's Church, Porthleven, we read: "Male person washed ashore. Name unknown"; while at Gunwalloe an entry is made: "1846. A lad's body, very much mangled. Three men, of the

awarded to ten or twelve Porthleven and Gunwalloe men for their gallantry on the day of the wreck. They received, besides, a present of about £50, which was divided amongst them. The letter is headed by a red wax seal, on which can be deciphered the words *Kongl Svenska och Norrska*.

"ROYAL SWEDISH AND NORWEGIAN
VICE CONSULATE,

PENZANCE, *22nd September*, 1847.

SIR,—I have great pleasure in informing you that His Majesty, the King of Norway, has been graciously pleased to direct me to convey to you his perfect satisfaction with the important services rendered by yourself and others in the preservation of Captain Niels Wuff Ellertsen, his mate, and two seamen, the only survivors of the crew of the Norwegian schooner, *Elisabeth*, of Bergen, unfortunately wrecked on the 20th day of November last, near Gunwalloe; and to present to you the accompanying testimonial, as a further acknowledgment of your bravery and good conduct.

"I have the honour to be, Sir,
"Your very obedient servant,
"RICHARD PEARCE,
"*Vice-Consul.*

"TO MR. RICHARD KITTO, PORTHLEVEN."

sprang into the breakers, and succeeded in throwing a line on board. His exploit adds another to the many noteworthy deeds of Porthleven men.

The trials, failures, and keen disappointments of a fisherman's life are comparatively unknown to the general public. The weary nights, the benumbed limbs, the cheerless watch under God's starlight, and straining glance through November fogs, are known too well by many Porthleven men. The dangers of the storm have to be encountered, but there is a great dread of the swiftly-moving ship or steamboat, the latter sometimes cutting the little fishing-boat in two, leaving the terror-stricken crew to struggle in the waves. The following incident will reveal the nature of the perils our brave fishermen are exposed to. We must, necessarily, contract the statements made by the sole survivor of the disaster, but could wish for more space to do greater justice to the narrative of his wonderful deliverance.

March 10th, 1871.—On Friday morning, March 10th, 1871, a Porthleven fishing-boat, named the *Desire*, left Falmouth Harbour for the Mount's Bay mackerel fishery. The crew consisted of the master, two lads (the skipper's sons), and five men. At

was settled, and the other hands turned into their little berths, where they were soon asleep, perhaps dreaming of the sights and sounds of Plymouth, whence they had recently sailed, and, probably, of loved ones not far away in their little native village of Porthleven. The watchman kept a sharp look-out, and did his best to peer through the haze that at intervals enveloped the *Desire*. He had little to fear from the S.S.W. breeze. The hours passed slowly away until about 11 o'clock, when a short, sharp cry startled the sleeping crew:—"All hands below on deck!" In a few moments the half-dressed, bewildered fishermen and the two frightened boys were on deck. What was their horror to behold a great iron ship of 1,700 tons rapidly nearing them! To escape was impossible; the destruction of the boat was inevitable. Crash! went the *Desire's* timbers before the *Corlic's* bows; and the fishing boat floated on the sea—in two halves. In the water, struggling for dear life, were the unfortunate fishermen and their young companions; and, alas! one after another they disappeared, exhausted and

overboard. Hanging from the forecastle of the *Corlic*, though quite unknown to the crew of the ship, was a single rope. This in the darkness he seized, and to this he despairingly clung. Dragged over and *under* the waves, onward he was pulled, but never relaxed his hold. A sailor on board the *Greenock* vessel had heard a crash, and climbed on the forecastle, from which he barely descried the young man's form. Seizing him by the back, he drew Strike into the *Corlic*, on whose deck he lay while the crew wondered at his deliverance. The rescued youth, exhausted as he was by his immersion, and suffering extreme anguish from a compound fracture, gave evidence of his earnest religious convictions. The astonished sailors heard him praise God for His mercy, and ascribe to Him his wonderful preservation. In the words of a brother fisherman who afterwards described the catastrophe in verse :—

> " His leg was broken with the wreck,
> Himself he tried to raise ;
> He struggled hard to get on deck ;
> To God he gave the praise."

CHAPTER V.

THE HARBOUR.

IN the summer of 1810 a prospectus was printed by W. Penaluna, Helston, and also by a Fleet Street firm. It related to the "Prince of Wales' Harbour, to be constructed at Porthleven." It stated: "The frequent occurrence of wrecks in the Mount's Bay, and the distressing calamities thereby produced on lives and property, have been a matter of serious reflection with many persons for some time past. Within a very short space of time, not less than twelve vessels have been lost near, and within sight of, the inhabitants of Porthleven." It proved, too, that surveys by competent engineers had been made of the cove, and it had been plainly demonstrated that a commodious, extensive, and safe harbour could be made. Such a haven would

could arrive from Mousehole and Newlyn—about eighteen miles westward—the nets were obliged to be taken up, and the fish abandoned, to save the boats. The latter, on such occasions, had to run to western ports, at a great risk, for want of a nearer shelter. Moreover, the proprietors of the fish secured were compelled to pay one-third of the catches as conveyance dues to the ports before mentioned—the only convenient *curing* places near. This would be saved by the construction of suitable curing-houses at Porthleven. Speculators were invited to become shareholders, with a prospect of its proving a profitable undertaking. The harbour would be easy of access, and its situation in the midst of an important mining district would secure a trade in coals, timber, and the like. From the decomposition of the felspar in the Tregoning Hill granite good china clay could be obtained for export; and besides, was there not a supply of the famous soap rock at hand—a mineral highly prized by the porcelain manufacturers? In cutting out the harbour basin there were great expectations of tin being found in the marshy bottom of the valley;

then Helston Mayor, and certain merchants of the same town, undertook the directorship until the Act of Incorporation was obtained. The sum of £30,000 was deemed sufficient for the formation of the harbour.

In 1811 an Act (51 Geo. III., c. 195) was passed for the construction of Porthleven Harbour. By this Act fourteen directors were appointed, eleven of whom were to hold at least ten shares of £100 each. Among the original Directors mentioned in it were five M.P.'s and two clergymen; these, with the remaining directors and fifteen others, constituted the original Porthleven Harbour Company. Their capital was to be £60,000, in shares of £50 or £100 each; and, if necessary, they were empowered to issue 300 new shares of £100 each. When half the capital was collected they were to commence building the pier. If the harbour were not completed in five years from the passing of the Act the latter would cease to have effect. The company were also entitled to levy (1) tonnage duties for the use of the harbour; (2) Duties on all goods imported and exported; (3) Duties on profits of salvage; (4) Wharfage duties. They could also raise money by borrowing, and

On the 18th October, 1825, the magistrates in quarter session assembled certified that Porthleven Harbour was completed to admit vessels of 200 tons, and in 1826 it was opened for traffic. The amount of capital and labour expended may be imagined when certain particulars are considered.

To remove the sandbar at the valley entrance was a considerable deed to accomplish. The construction of a strong granite pier, built on the rock, and extending into the sea, prevented the reaccumulation of the gravel. The shingle was wheeled in barrows by seventy workmen, and upset on the eastern side of the pier. The latter is 465 feet long, 26 feet high, and 21 feet wide, and is well able to withstand the force of the huge waves that the winter storms hurl against it. As first attempted, the pier was built from the shore outward; but the waves washed the masonry away. But under the direction of a Mr. Pearce, of Sheerness, the arrangement of the work was reversed, the building being commenced outside and then shoreward. The new plan proved successful.

At an expense of nearly £200,000 the harbour has been prepared for the reception of vessels of from 200 to 400 tons burden. There is a basin,

or narrowest part (between the jetties), is about 100 feet. The contents of the basin are:—Width at south end, next the jetties, about 230 feet; at north end 360 feet length, north to south, 720 feet. Harbour and basin comprise about 28 statute acres. The sum of £8,000 was paid by the company to purchase the land and old houses required in forming the roads, basin, etc. It would be interesting to trace the varied changes in the history of Porthleven Harbour. One company after another attempted to establish a trade, and to raise a revenue. Now we read of mortgage; afterwards of borrowed loans from the Exchequer Loan Commissioners. Twice it was advertised for sale, by public auction or by private treaty, but "nobody would have the harbour at any price." The income derived from boats and vessels as Harbour Dues from 1816 to 1830 amounted to about £92 per annum. Debts were incurred by the Company, and the harbour master's salary was sadly in arrear. But in 1855 the interest in the harbour became vested in an enterprising firm—

water from the neighbouring mines was diverted by a culvert, and by preparing grooves, in which balks of timber were let down during stormy weather, the boats and shipping could remain secure during the severest gale. As a result of their exertions, the trade of the port and the prosperity of the fishermen greatly increased.

By the Act of Incorporation, the original promoters were empowered to levy certain rates and duties on articles imported and exported. From a perusal of the Schedules of the Act of 1869, we notice that the dues per ton of vessels frequenting the port, provide for ships of 120 tons and upwards. To import or export a *hawk* requires a levy of twopence, while for a *bag of feathers* the rate is ninepence. A *side of bacon* can be sent out for a due of sixpence, but a *dining-table* necessitates the payment of a fourpenny impost.

Apart from the steamer or sailing vessel, that may be frequently seen in the harbour, there is a more lively scene presented when the fleet of fishing-boats is preparing for sea, or leaving the basin. Their brown sails present a pleasing sight, and by contrast tend to increase the charm of the blue summer sea, while

fishing for *mackerel* was made, when the late Mr. Thomas Jacka had a boat built for that branch of the fishery. One Friday afternoon, about twelve years later, the little fleet of Porthleven boats, mostly of small size, proceeded to sea, with every promise of a fine night. The weather was mild, and the wind, if any, was "off the land." They had not gone long before the sky became overcast, and the wind increased to a hurricane. What would become of the boats? Not one came into harbour that night. They were scattered hither and thither. All night long there were weeping and loud cries heard in the village for absent fathers, sons, and husbands. Yet no life was lost. One boat reached Mullion, and the occupants were hauled by ropes up the cliff, but with faces so battered that their relatives failed to recognize them on their return. Most of the boats reached Porthleven in safety, though some of the men were so weak from exposure, that they had to be assisted to their homes. The *Ark* was unheard of for a fortnight, when news was received from the crew, who had been taken to Rotterdam, whence in due time they arrived at Porthleven. For many years an annual Thanksgiving Service was held in the old

In 1848, sixty-three boats, of all sizes, belonged to the port. About twenty were engaged in the mackerel fishery. Perhaps it will not be uninteresting if we select a few names from the list of the old fishing-fleet, all gone at the present time with one or two exceptions. Shall we attempt a classification?

BIRDS: Dove, Lark. PLANTS AND TREES: Pink, Olive, Laurel, Vine. VARIOUS: Ant, Drone, Pilchard, Beehive!

Besides the mackerel fishery, the boats are engaged in fishing for herrings, pilchards, and in the shell-fishery. Hook-and-line fishing is also vigorously prosecuted. The largest sized boats are among the finest modelled and best equipped in the kingdom. Most, if not all, have been built on the *Bank*, at the northern head of the inner basin at Porthleven. One local builder has just launched his fifteenth boat. When setting out for the Scotch herring-grounds, or for the Plymouth mackerel season, they are well manned and provisioned. They have excellent sailing qualities, and are capable of enduring great stress of weather. Being fitted with every con-

the commencement of the Plymouth season. The sale realized about £3,000. This result, in the time, is the most remarkable on record at Porthleven. The whole were secured in about a fortnight. The smaller class boats are employed in the pilchard drift fishery, as before intimated. These, with the "hookers" and "crabbers," may frequently be seen returning from the deep with a goodly burden of silvery fish, or with well-filled mawn of crabs, crayfish, or lobsters.

Connected with the pilchard fishery is the system of fish-curing. When the catches are large, and when the demand is consequently less, with a corresponding diminution in prices, the fish are not put into the market, but are taken into port and carried in baskets, etc., to the fish cellars. Here they are "huddled" in heaps, mixed with salt, and after three or four weeks transferred into the casks or hogsheads (loc. *hosgeds*). After a large percentage of their oil has been pressed out, the pilchards are ready for shipment to the Mediterranean markets. This fish-curing time is an occasion of activity amongst the

provided with his outfit: how is this secured? To screen his body from piercing winds, loving fingers are busy knitting a strong, warm worsted frock or jersey, also long comfortable stockings. But worsted is a poor shelter from the drenching spray and driving rain, so there is a demand on the females for the supply of other garments. A "jumper" is made of "duck," and over both is the "oiler," a covering of "unbleached" made waterproof. For his head there is a "sou'-wester" of oiled cloth, well padded inside with flannel; while strong "sea-boots," reaching to his thighs, complete his usual costume. Besides the making and mending of the clothing, there are nets to be provided and repaired. Here, too, the women and elder girls render great assistance. Mesh after mesh is formed by practised hands, until the net is finished. Sometimes a huge rent, made by the vessel or torn by the "dogs" (dog-fish), requires their patient attention, while father is busy "barking" his new mackerel net, tarring his boat, or oiling his boots, and while brother is making a crab-pot of wicker-work. Besides the individual efforts of the family to provide the necessary nets, machine power has

girls, travellers, or clerks, in this important industry. A visit to the works reveals the nature and amount of the business transacted. The various processes can be traced whereby the American cotton becomes converted into the finished net, ready for immediate use. In addition to the ordinary sea-fishery nets, Mr. Eddy manufactures salmon, aviary, and horticultural netting and shading, as well as conservatory blinds and lawn-tennis nets. His travellers visit the most important ports and towns of England, while his business transactions extend over the United Kingdom.

Before leaving the description of our fisherman and his occupation, we would add a word or two in regard to his general character. He is sturdily honest, and has won more than a local reputation for strict sobriety and orderly conduct. His encounters with the storm and the billows have given him that daring intrepidity which is the boast of our British seafaring population. Towards his family his tenderness is marked, while his love of home is proverbial. He is eminently loyal,—as was demonstrated by the reception given to H.R.H. the Duke of Edinburgh, while on a visit to the Coast Guard

CHAPTER VI.

GROWTH OF METHODISM.

AMONGST the old folks there is a belief that Wesley visited Porthleven about 1789. The first Methodist sermon was preached in the village about this date. To hear the glad tidings, the people assembled in a fish-cellar or fish-loft (perhaps both). Seated on nets, oars, masts, coils of rope, casks, sails, etc., they listened attentively while the veteran preacher proclaimed God's love to the erring and the fallen. The Gospel net enclosed many, and several were led to serve the Lord.

The gracious influence was extended, and the fish-cellar and loft became too small to accommodate the increasing numbers who were desirous of meet-

Society was without organisation, having no regular provision for the conduct of services. Several persons visited Helston and the neighbouring hamlets for the sake of attending the Class-meeting, and from these scattered villages parties came to assist at the Porthleven services. The little company was occasionally favoured with a visit from one of the few local preachers then found in the county. Tradition asserts that a Mr. Hammill, of Helston, was the first visitor to the port in that capacity; it is affirmed that his ministry was valued and blessed of God.

Sometimes large catches of fish occupied most of the available space of the cellar; on such occasions the services had to be conducted elsewhere. Preacher and people had to seek some other retreat: this was usually found in the *Long Room*. The latter was *the* room of the village, and within its walls, long since demolished, many strange scenes have been enacted. It adjoined the old public-house, already referred to, and was the place of resort on the occasion of village festivals and *court* days. There the folks met to-

a piece of candle would be rubbed over the bow-string, and the puzzled performer would try in vain to draw musical sounds from the greasy strings. In the public-house, too, a deserter was shot by an officer from Pendennis Castle one winter's morn; and the bullet-mark can still be seen. An old man yet lives, who remembers, when a boy, listening at the Long Room door to catch the sound of the dying man's groans. And here on the Sabbath the congregations met to thank God for His goodness, and to plead for His guidance. The assemblies gradually increased, until a bold project was suggested: why could they not build a chapel? The cellar, loft, and Long Room were well filled by regular attenders week after week. The time had come to build a suitable sanctuary.

In the congregation was a certain individual, who, if not a member of the Society, yet took an active interest in the scheme. In conjunction with the late Mr. Lanyon, of Helston, he set to work to raise the funds. Money was procured, but not enough. It was thought the balance might be borrowed. Accord-

chapel can be turned into a dwellin' 'ouse!" Without doubt this was quite business-like in his estimation.

About 1800 the first Methodist chapel in Porthleven was built. (Our illustration shows all that remains of the historic edifice.) The building was soon filled during both the week-night meetings and the Sunday services. One great want was experienced; a good class-leader was not to be had until 1810-11. Then Mr. Lanyon gathered the first class together, commencing with five or six persons. They met in the chapel on the Sabbath morning, or during the week-nights. Soon the class numbered twenty—a little band of believers whose names are recorded on earth, and, we trust, written in heaven. We hope to give a list elsewhere.

In five years a need to enlarge the chapel was felt. The same individuals who arranged for building planned the enlargement. The people responded to the call. Some brought the stone, others dug the foundation. One party supplied the timber, while another built the walls. They "had a mind to work," and at little cost the alteration was effected. A

FIRST WESLEYAN-METHODIST CHAPEL : PRESENT REMAINS.

and in 1815, with hymns of thanksgiving, the enlarged chapel was opened for worship.

Previous to 1815 the Sunday School children had been brought together in the Long Room, but their instruction was not properly provided for. Their meeting interfered with the preaching services, and *vice versâ*. But when the children betook themselves to the newly-enlarged chapel, their meetings were regularly held, and the teaching systematically arranged. Teachers and officials were appointed. The late Misses Rogers, of Penrose, took a lively interest in this Sabbath School. Communicants, as they were, of the Church of England, they nobly united with these few early Methodists in their attempts to train the young in the fear of the Lord. As teachers, they attended regularly, and by gifts of money and books rendered invaluable assistance. It was from this old chapel the scholars started on their march to Sithney church, the account of which may be seen in a former chapter.

Steadily and surely Methodism was growing in the district, when, in 1824, there occurred a great ingathering of the people. In that year there was

words of Walter Lawry, one of the preachers in the Circuit, the people in the chapel on Sundays "were like pilchards in bulk." Often two lines of persons might have been seen at one form, taking turns to sit. For want of air the candles often went out! On one occasion a chair was brought to assist the preacher to reach the window and thereby enter the chapel; there was no possibility of pushing through the congregation. As a result of this spiritual visitation, there was a marked increase in the classes and in the number of leaders.

In addition to the Wesleyan-Methodist Society, the Bible Christians had also, about this period, gathered a congregation together. According to some their services took place in the Long Room, and, from the "heaving-stock" near, John Bassett, of Tavistock (?), was the first to preach to the people. About fifty-five years ago their first chapel was built. This was a providential circumstance, there being room for all to worship. If the pulpit of the Wesleyan chapel were occupied by some famous preacher, such as Dick Hampden, and the people were shut out for want of room, they could find a seat in the Bible Christian sanctuary; or if the latter were

enlarged. It was to this old building, since removed, that Florence Hosking, the lame cripple, repaired one summer Sunday, believing that God was about to heal her infirmity. The readers of "The King's Son" are aware that her faith was effectual, and by the blessing of her heavenly Father she returned home *without* the aid of her crutches. This happened in 1844. We may note that the son who caused her lameness died at Porthleven during the early part of February of the present year.

In 1863 the present Bible Christian chapel was constructed at a cost of £500, to seat 400 worshippers. At an outlay of £330 more, in 1876, seat room was secured for an additional 300 people by enlarging the building. The Society added a commodious Sunday School room and vestry in 1879, at an outlay of £700. The present number of members is about 250, and the Sabbath School is well attended. The Porthleven chapel is in the Breage Circuit, in which there are five other places of worship belonging to the Society.

Meanwhile, as the years passed away, it was seen that Wesleyan-Methodism was progressing, and becoming a plant of vigorous growth. To seat or

poor, and a bold scheme was soon presented to them for consideration. Some of the more zealous of their number proposed the construction of a new chapel—larger, better ventilated, and more commodious. In the initiation of this enterprise, the late Tobias Rowe, John Waters, and William Richards took a prominent part. Appeals were made for help; methods for securing funds were devised, while sceptical onlookers grumbled, "What do they want of such a chapel as that down to Pourtleben?" By degrees the work was commenced, and, in 1840, the second Wesleyan-Methodist chapel in Porthleven was opened for Divine worship, and the people thanked the Lord for His goodness.

The following year—24th August, 1841—St. Bartholomew's Church, Porthleven, was consecrated. Under an Order in Council, 1844, the limits of Porthleven Ecclesiastical District were defined. The first vicar appointed was the Rev. Lampriere, who was succeeded by the Revs. Griffith, C. Hartley, and T. L. Williams; the latter clergyman was admitted to the living in 1851, and continues to hold it. The first marriage was solemnized in 1847, while in 1848 the first burial occurred, October

terment of bodies washed ashore or found at sea —*e.g.*, "February 9th, 1862. Male person found at sea. Name unknown." The church has seat accommodation for 300, and its day and Sunday Schools are well attended.

For twenty-eight years the Wesleyan chapel continued to be well filled on ordinary occasions. During the interval between the construction of the first chapel and the period to which we refer, many of the old folks had been gathered home, and other voices mingled in the sanctuary or were heard in the prayer-meeting. Other ministers visited the Society; other leaders conducted the classes. As the population increased, there was a demand for seats in the Chapel. It soon became apparent that an enlargement must be made to meet the new requirements: accordingly two recesses or wings were added to the right and left of the rostrum. This alteration was effected in 1867-8.

Porthleven formed a portion of the Helston Wesleyan Circuit at this time, and both ministers and local preachers experienced great inconvenience in fulfilling their appointments. Some of the chapels were many miles from the Circuit head, and the

the Conference had decided that the third Circuit minister should reside at Porthleven; but this advantage was insufficient to meet the needs of the growing Society. At the quarterly and district meetings the question of the Division of the Circuit was vigorously debated, and was eventually referred to the decision of Conference. That body placed the matter before the lay representatives, and by them the arrangement was approved and sanctioned. So in 1878, under the able administration of the Rev. E. Dodds, Porthleven became the head of the Porthleven Wesleyan-Methodist Circuit. In 1879 the Society built and furnished for their minister a commodious preacher's house.

The new Circuit embraces seven places of worship—viz., Porthleven, Sithney, Breage, Carleen, Hendra, Ashton, and Chynhale chapels. The latter was built about the time of the Circuit division, and opened by the late Dr. Punshon. It is near Trevarno, the mansion of W. Bickford-Smith, Esq., J.P., to whose liberality the elegant little chapel owes its erection. From the surrounding district a Society and congre-

Sithney and Breage were frequently mentioned by Wesley, and his visits to them and records of such visitations constitute an interesting page in the history of local Methodism. The other chapels are well attended, and have proved a blessing to the district.

On June 8th, 1881, an important ceremony took place in Porthleven. The foundation stones of a third Wesleyan chapel were laid. On the occasion referred to there was a vast gathering of people from various parts of the county. In the morning the Rev. R. Roberts, of Liverpool, preached in the "old" chapel (of 1840). After a public luncheon the centre of interest was the site of the new chapel, where hundreds had assembled to witness the stone-laying. In the evening, after tea, a public meeting was held in the old chapel, presided over by S. D. Waddy, Esq., Q.C.; and in the Bible Christian chapel a sermon was preached by the Rev. R. Roberts. The net sum of £224 was realized during the day, of which the Sunday School contributed £34. The following gentlemen laid foundation stones: Messrs. W. Bickford-Smith, John Holman,

the District, preached; and in the evening the gifted minister from Liverpool again preached to a vast congregation. The opening services were continued for a month, when the following preachers ministered to large and appreciative audiences:—Revs. G. Bowden (Bristol); J. H. Brown (Plymouth); Dr. Rigg (Ex-President of the Conference); and E. Dodds, who had left his Yorkshire manse to visit his Porthleven and Circuit friends.

The new building is a prominent structure in the Gothic style, and for its architectural beauty is deservedly admired. The interior is fitted with every convenience suited to modern requirements. Galleries and pews are of pitch pine, polished and varnished. There is a large front window of great beauty, and the rostrum is chastely carved. The comfort of minister and worshipper has been studied, and, what is of far greater importance, the preaching of the Word is regularly provided for. The total membership of the Porthleven Society at present is 315, and the building will accommodate about 800. A second

CHAPTER VII.

PORTHLEVEN PRESENT.

ST. PETER'S DAY, June 29th, is Porthleven's annual festival. In the olden time Midsummer Day was the great day of the year, when a fair, attended by pleasure-seekers from the surrounding towns and villages, was held in the little port, all bent on boating or other pastime. That this was the case, the following extract from the Helston parish registers will show: "1788, June 24th. About five o'clock p.m., a Porthleven boat, sailing on a party of pleasure towards Mullion Gull Rock, was upset (by what accident is unknown) about one-and-a-half

while terraces and boats in harbour will wear a pleasing appearance. In the bay outside boating parties may be noticed, enjoying a trip on the blue sea. On cliffs and along the beach stragglers will be found inhaling the Atlantic breeze, while on the summer air comes the laughter of the happy children. Lodging-houses are full, but each home is an impromptu restaurant, where friend and stranger are welcome. In the afternoon the children of the Sunday School, preceded by a brass band, and attended by their teachers, perambulate the thoroughfares, and march through gardens, singing hymns at intervals, and picturing their treat of cake and tea in the Harbour Company's timber yard. A bazaar or local exhibition of arts and industries proves attractive to the adults, whose appetites, sharpened by the bracing sea air, have doubtless been satisfied. Towards evening the din of drums, and the shrill whistle of the merry-go-round from the Bank, indicate the showman's whereabouts. The throng of pleasure-lovers grows inconveniently denser, until locomotion is a matter of difficulty. Night throws

lifeboat, each ready for immediate use in such a circumstance as the catastrophe of 1788.

But perhaps the reader does not appreciate the bustle of a fair, or the pushing of a crowd, and would prefer a quieter occasion to make Porthleven's acquaintance. Inducements can be offered to such. If in search of health or relaxation from business worries, the visitor will be amply rewarded by a temporary or permanent residence. As long ago as 1810, Porthleven was highly recommended as a health resort :—"The valetudinarian and invalid will have little occasion to travel to Italy or the south of France to find a mild and salubrious climate, the peculiarity of the situation being such as to be sheltered by surrounding hills from the bleak winds, and having the advantage of being in the vicinity of Penrose (the seat of John Rogers, Esq.), a finely-wooded and picturesque scenery, which affords many interesting subjects to the landscape painter, and by the erection of convenient and accommodating machines, *it may vie with, if not excel, any of the*

mands a sea-view of great magnificence. Taking the last twenty-one years, the percentage of the prevalent winds at Porthleven and in the neighbourhood has been:—S.W., 22·07; W., 10·6; N., 17; N.E. 13·8; S., 9; S.E., 9·4; N.W., 13·22; and last, the trying E., 4·55. The delicate patient would be saved from exposure to the more severe winds of this table.

The scientific observer will not fail to find abundant material for investigation. The geologist will be delighted to examine the junction of the granite and clay slate at Trewavas, westward of Porthleven. He will notice the contrast in colour, and proceeding eastward will follow the clay-slate, and trace quartz veins and trap dykes in the cliff face. Nearer Mullion he will find greenstone, conglomerate, and the far-famed serpentine. Wandering on the shores of the Loe Pool, he will accept the theory that the lake was once an inlet of Mount's Bay, and will discern in the pool's perpendicular sides something more than the action of the Loe in a storm. He may receive the data, formulated by a scientist, that the land, inside a line drawn from Trewavas Head to Gunwalloe, being destroyed, the slate-mud deposit

formation, as has been already suggested. He will be interested to learn that from borings made in the Loe Bar layers of silt and fine sand, as well as coarse gravel, were found, the whole resting on a floor of clay-slate or quartz. At one spot the boring tool cut through rotten trees and pieces of wood; and on the east side no bottom to the sand was reached at fifty-one feet.

Rambling along the lanes, up Methleigh Valley, around the shores of the Loe, or through wooded Penrose, the botanist will discover many a rare plant. In the valley he will be charmed with the abundance of Osmunda, while in Duft's Hole—an old adit on the west of the Pool—he will find a rich display of *Asplenium marinum.* One little plant—*Corrigiola littoralis*—changes its habitat from one side of the Loe to the other. At Carminow Creek, an eastward expansion of the lake, many choice plants may be gathered—*e.g., Chenopodium botryoides, Elatine hexandra*, etc.

The beach after a storm, and the rock-pools at low

drawn on the beach, may be seen curious creatures from the deep—monk-fish, electric-ray, or angler-fish; while the trawl reveals amongst its spoils sea-mice, and the forbidding-looking octopus, a good specimen of which was shown us a few days ago (March 10th). Rare birds have also been shot in the neighbourhood, among which have been a Golden Oriole, Ring Ousel, Spoonbill, Hooper Swan, and Fork-tailed Petrel.

For the ordinary visitor Porthleven has its attractions. A ramble to the western cliffs (with a passing call to inspect the varied treasures of the little museum of F. Penberthy, Esq.) will give him an opportunity of seeing the seaport at a glance. On the right rise the rugged crags near the Land's End, and eastward Halzephron and Pradannack rear their storm-stained heads. Under his feet are the remains, here and there, of drowned sailors, lost on the rocks below. Yonder, on the right, is Penzance and its neighbouring villages; and on the left are the hamlets of the Lizard peninsula. In the offing, sparkling in the noontide sunshine, gleam the white sails of the homeward-bound trader, while against the horizon

and soon, as the darkness deepens, the lights increase in brightness, until they look like the illuminations of a mighty, distant city. Returning from his wanderings, the tourist will attend to the wants of the inner man, and will, perhaps, desire to know how the great world, far away from this quiet retreat, is progressing. There is nothing easier. Let him step into the Bickford-Smith Scientific and Literary Institute, and he will find morning and evening telegrams from the great metropolis sent hither twice a day.

The Institute owes its erection to the beneficence of him whose name it justly bears. The building is a handsome structure, and from it a magnificent view may be obtained of Mount's Bay. The reading-room is 40 feet by 20 feet, and is fitted with pitch pine dadoing, and warmed by two stoves. The massive oak tables are well supplied with the London and provincial papers, as well as magazines and reviews. The Lending and Reference Library will contain a carefully selected assortment of books to suit general

and also as a second guiding light; the first, standing on the pier head, shows a red light, and both are much valued. In the reading-room, lectures, classes, and entertainments are frequently held, and are well attended by the majority of the members. It must be a source of pleasure to Mr. Bickford-Smith to know that his generous gift is so much appreciated by young and old. The Institute, costing about £2,000, was opened on December 17th, 1884.

Attention has lately been directed to the sanitary condition of Porthleven, and an engineer and Government inspector have visited the port, to prepare plans and institute an inquiry respecting the proposed water-supply and drainage system. When these works have been accomplished, other improvements will doubtless follow. Among the requirements of the little town we might suggest a few. There is a lack of bathing facilities. A beach could be formed on the western side of the harbour by removing the rocks. This would be effected by the aid of dynamite or similar explosive. On the beach thus prepared bathing-machines might be stationed, and the whole arrangements for their control, and the use of the bathing beach, invested in a local bathing-board.

APPENDIX I.

WRECKS AT OR NEAR PORTHLEVEN, 1807—1810, AND 1859—1884.

1807—1810.

Vessel.	Tonnage.	Drowned.	General Remarks.
s and Rebecca, Transport; Rochester	400	41	Value, above £30,000.
Frigate *Anson*, Captain Lydiard	400	About 50	,, 80,000.
an and August Recovery. Corbett, master	110	9	,, 20,000.
Vife		Total loss.	,, 2,000.
May, master	103		,, 1,000.
Cunningham, master	500		,, 20,000.
da, West-Indiaman		Total loss.	,, 60,000.
Ann, West-Indiaman. Tongue, ter		,,	,, 60,000.
nish Brig		,,	,, 10,000.
Clio. Marshall, master		,,	,, 8,000.

ships totally lost, names unknown.

1859—1884.

Liverpool	1894	4	Cargo—Cannel coal.
rtmouth	219		Crew saved. Cargo, railway iron.
Sunderland	325	2	Ran ashore at entrance of Porthleven Harbour. Two silver medals granted to Porthleven men. Crew saved by rocket apparatus.
ling, of Yarmouth, Nova	1553		
ver, of Sunderland	299	(supposed) 10	} All hands drowned.
f Tremblade	77		Crew saved by Coastguards and others.
Ann, of Plymouth	44		Wreck near Porthleven Pier. Crew saved.
ellegina, a Dutch galliot	59		Cargo—Beans. Crew saved.
enzance	81		Got ashore Harbour entrance. Crew saved.
usa	381	3	Cargo—logwood, from Hayti.

r 1807 to November 1810 the loss of property exceeded £300,000, with upwards of in the immediate vicinity of Porthleven. "Had there existed a Harbour in the , the whole might have been saved."—*Prospectus of the Prince of Wales' tructed at Porthleven, Mount's Bay, Cornwall.*

APPENDIX II.

PORTHLEVEN HARBOUR CONSTRUCTION.

(A) Receipts and Expenditure 1811—May 22nd, 1814.

	£	s.	d.		£	s.	d.
Received from Proprietors under Company's Act	22,374	19	10	Surveys, and soliciting Incorporation Act	2,547	6	3
Received from Loan of Mr. Richard	2,000	0	0	Soliciting New Act	386	17	1
Received from Rents at the Harbour	45	12	6	Earthwork, Masonry, Stone, Timber, Labour, Salaries, etc.	11,159	2	4
				Purchases of Estates within Harbour limits, Int. on Loan	6,574	0	0
				Cash in hands of Director of works (A. Blair, Esq.) and Treasurer	3,753	6	8
	24,420	12	4		24,420	12	4

(*Signed*) T. G. VANDER GUCHT,
Clerk to the Company.

(B) *Extracts from Captain Blair's Report of Progress of the Work, April 20th, 1814.*

Pier:—Carried out with nearly 74,870 cubic feet firm masonry, consisting of moorstone and granite, connected by excellent mortar, composed of Aberthaw lime and iron-stone sand, and tree-nailed where thought necessary. Total expense £11,870. To prevent return of sand and gravel 1,100 tons more stone required. Cost £2,310. During last winter in strong southerly gales a very small quantity of gravel appeared to have been washed over the lower part of it. One of the pier stones during S.W. gales was raised from its place by the force of the sea, and carried to a distance of 56 feet. It weighed 1 ton $18\frac{1}{2}$ cwt.

Gravel removed:—
   (*a*) From Channel. Space 400 feet by 300 feet and 7 feet deep, 40,000 tons. Cost £300.
   (*b*) From interior channel, 100 feet long: 30 av. breadth: 14 feet deep. £200 cost.

Warehouse nearly completed:—56 feet long, 25 feet wide, three storeys high. This formed winter employment for the masons, and part of the labourers. Worth £800.

Excavated space near Warehouse. For Coal Yard. Stone used for facing wharves.

Work to be done to suit 50 *Vessels of* 200 *Tons each.*

Ground excavations:—1,200 feet × 250 feet × 28 feet = 8,400,000 cubic feet, or 381,814 tons. Cost £4,772.

Posts, Rings, Chains, and Cranes to be fixed. Cost £500.

Wharves to be constructed. Local stone—lime only upper part—to be faced with moorstone.

Basin. For future consideration.

A little *Tin* has been found in the excavations; more is expected. Tin-streaming was tried here about twenty

JOHN HARRIS, THE CORNISH POET:

THE STORY OF HIS LIFE;

BY HIS SON,

J. HOWARD HARRIS.

With Portrait.   Crown 8vo.   Cloth extra.

Price One Shilling.

PRESS NOTICES.

Western Morning News.—"The little memoir deserves a large circulation. Extremely well brought before the reader."

Penryn Advertiser.—"A cheap edition of the poet's life has been ably rendered by his eldest son."

Falmouth Times.—"We were not able to let down this book, after once opening its pages, before reading it through; it is an intensely interesting story of an intensely interesting character. . . . Handsome little volume . . . possesses simple beauty and reality."

Western Antiquary.—"This little work is truly a labour of love, and one cannot peruse its pages without perceiving the loving nature of the labour. . . . The son has woven the threads of his lamented father's life into a story which is romantic, though true, and eminently real, though full of poetic passages."

Christian World.—"We are glad that so pleasing a memoir of a brave man and a true poet should be produced."

CLASSIFIED CATALOGUE

OF

New and Popular Works,

PUBLISHED BY

S. W. PARTRIDGE & Co., 9, Paternoster Row,

LONDON.

Seven Shillings and Sixpence.

Providence of God Illustrated. By the Author of "History in all Ages." With numerous full-page Illustrations. Large Crown 8vo., 296 pages. Cloth gilt, gilt edges.

Memorials of the Wesley Family. By G. J. Stevenson, M.A. Prepared chiefly from Original Documents, and including Historical Biographies of the Leading Members of the Wesley Family for nearly 250 years. With Genealogical Table of the Family from A.D. 938, to the year 1875, and Photographic Group of 15 Portraits. Demy 8vo., cloth   (Morocco, 10s. 6d.)

"The most complete and reliable account of the Wesley family ever presented to the world."—*Christian.*

The Two Babylons; or, the Papal Worship proved to be the Worship of Nimrod and his Wife. With 61 Illustrations from Nineveh, Babylon, Egypt, Pompeii, &c. By the Rev. A. Hislop. Sixth Edition. Crown 8vo.

"Clearly proves that the religion of the Church of Rome is the religion of Babylon, tinted and varnished with the name of Christianity."—*Achill Herald.*

Five Shillings.

Aileen Aroon: A Memoir. With other tales of Faithful Friends and Favourites, sketched from the life. By Gordon Stables, C.M.,

Five Shillings—Continued.

Our Zoological Friends; or, Conversations of an Uncle with his Nephews and Nieces about Animals, &c. By Harland Coultas. Cloth. Illustrated.

Animals and their Young. By the same Author. Cloth. Illustrated.

Our Dumb Companions: or, Conversations about Dogs, Horses, Donkeys, &c. Illustrated.

Grace Ashleigh's Life-work. By Mrs. Mary D. R. Boyd. Full-page Illustrations, cloth.

Uncle John's Anecdotes of Animals and Birds. With several full-page Engravings. Cloth.

Uncle John's Picture Book for his Young Friends. With 140 full-page Engravings, by first-class Artists, and letterpress by Miss Tupper. Cloth.

My Darling's Picture Book. With full-page Engravings by Harrison Weir, &c. Cloth.

Ritualism; Romanism; and the Reformation; a Question of Fact. By Samuel Wainwright, D.D., Author of "Christian Certainty," &c. Large Post 8vo., cloth.

Four Shillings.

Walks through Picture Land. 140 full-page Engravings. Cloth.

Happy Moments in Picture Land. 140 full-page Engravings. Cloth.

Three Shillings and Sixpence.

Mark Desborough's Vow. A Tale. By Annie S. Swan, author of "Grandmother's Child," etc. Crown 8vo., cloth extra. Illustrated.

The Better Part. A Tale. By Annie S. Swan, author of

Three Shillings and Sixpence—*Continued.*

A Bunch of Cherries, gathered and strung by J. W. Kirton. With Illustrations. Cloth.

Morning Dewdrops; or, the Young Abstainer. By Mrs. C. L. Balfour. A Revised and Illustrated Edition of this most valuable Temperance Book for the Young. Cloth.

Learned in the Law. Sketches of Eminent Lawyers. By W. H. Davenport Adams. Crown 8vo., cloth, bevelled, lettered, gilt edges.

Mick Tracy, the Irish Scripture Reader. With Engravings. Fifteenth Thousand. Crown 8vo., cloth.

"A tale of interest, with adventure enough for a three volume novel."—*Irish Ecclesiastical Gazette.*

Tim Doolan, The Irish Emigrant. By same author. With Frontispiece. Fifth Thousand. Crown 8vo., cloth.

"We predict for 'Tim Doolan' a wide and lasting fame."—*Weekly Times.*

Gathered Grain, consisting of Select Extracts from the Best Authors. Edited by E. A. H. Fourth Edition. Crown 8vo., cloth.

The Brandens; or, Workers in a Neglected Service. By Eliza Hutchinson, author of "Our Neighbour," &c. Illustrations. Crown 8vo., cloth.

"A well told and instructive story."—*Rock.*

The Bible and Temperance; or, the True Scriptural Basis of the Temperance Movement. By Rev. Thomas Pearson. Crown 8vo., cloth.

"A book that will repay the cost of attentive perusal."—*Watchman.*

Three People. A Story of the American Crusade. Small 4to., cloth. 29 Full-page Engravings.

Stories of Irish Life. By H. Martin. Small 4to., cloth.

Three Shillings.

Bible Picture Roll. Containing a large Engraving of a Scripture subject, with letterpress for each day in the month. With colored cover.

Children's Picture Roll. Consisting of 21 Illustrated Leaves.

Two Shillings and Sixpence.

Teresa's Secret. By Laura M. Lane, author of "Gentleman Verschoyle," "My Sister's Keeper," "A Dresden Romance," etc., etc. Illustrated. Crown 8vo. Cloth extra.

Clovie and Madge. A Tale. By Mrs. G. S. Reaney, author of "Our Daughters," "Found at Last," etc. Crown 8vo., cloth extra. Illustrated.

The Gipsy Queen. By Emma Leslie, author of "The Water Waifs," etc. Crown 8vo., cloth extra. Illustrated.

A Red Brick Cottage. By Lady Hope, author of "Our Coffee Room," etc. Crown 8vo., cloth, gilt.

Cloudland; or, the Secret of Usefulness and Happiness. Fcap. 4to., cloth. Full-page Engravings.

Arthur Egerton's Ordeal; or, God's Ways not Our Ways. By E. Leslie. With full-page Engravings. Fcap. 4to., cloth.

True Riches; or, Wealth without Wings. By T. S. Arthur. With several Illustrations. Cloth.

Temperance Stories for the Young. By T. S. Arthur, author of "Ten Nights in a Bar Room." With seven full-page Engravings. Fcap. 4to., cloth.

Nature's Mighty Wonders. By the Rev. Dr. Newton. Cloth.

Rays from the Sun of Righteousness. By the Rev. Dr. Newton. With numerous Illustrations. Cloth.

Safe Compass, and how it Points. By the Rev. Dr. Newton. With numerous Illustrations. Cloth.

Our Four-footed Friends; or, the History of Manor Farm, and the People and Animals there. By Mary Howitt. With numerous Illustrations. Fcap. 4to., cloth.

The Brook's Story, and other Tales for the Young. By Mrs. Bowen. Fcap. 4to., cloth.

Edith Oswald; or, Living for Others. By Jane M. Kippin, author of "Aunt Margaret's Visit," &c. With Illustrations. Cloth.

Gerard Mastyn; or, the Son of a Genius. By E. H. Burrage. With Illustrations. Cloth.

How a Farthing made a Fortune; or, "Honesty is the Best Policy." By Mrs. C. E. Bowen. With seven full-page Engravings. Cloth.

Hubert Ellerdale. A Tale of the Days of Wycliffe. By W. Oak Rhind. With Illustrations. Cloth.

Two Shillings and Sixpence—*Continued.*

The King's Highway. By the Rev. Dr. Newton. With numerous Illustrations. Cloth.

Lil Grey; or, Arthur Chester's Courtship. By Mrs. E. Beavan. Frontispiece. Crown 8vo., cloth.

"Suitable for every Temperance library."—*Templar's Watchword.*

Sire and Son; a Startling Contrast. A Temperance Tale. By Rev. Amos White. With Engravings. Crown 8vo., cloth.

"This well-told narrative ought to have a mission amongst moderate drinkers."—*Christian.*

The Royal Rights of the Lord Jesus. By the Rev. W. Leask, D.D. Crown 8vo., cloth.

Happy Years at Hand; Outlines of the Coming Theocracy. By the same author. Second Thousand. Crown 8vo., cloth.

The Beauties of the Bible. Third edition. By the same author. Fcap. 8vo., cloth.

Counsels and Knowledge from the Words of Truth. By the Rev. F. Whitfield, Vicar of St. Mary's, Hastings. Second edition. Crown 8vo., cloth, gilt.

The Hero of Danzig; or, Konrad the Standard Bearer. By Ferd. Sonnenburg. Translated with the Author's permission by LUIGI, author of "Legends of the Rhine, for Children," "Nanta," etc. Imperial 16mo., cloth, gilt edges, lettered, with Six Engravings.

Cuthberht of Lindisfarne. His Life and Times. By Alfred C. Fryer, F.R.H.S. Crown 8vo., cloth.

"A book Churchmen and Antiquaries will delight to read."—*Derbyshire Courier.*

Crumbs from Dame Nature's Table. By Mrs. Alfred W. Adams. With Illustrations. Second edition. Royal 16mo., cloth.

"The sentiment of the book is pleasant, refined, and healthy, and full of true religious feeling. It contains a great deal of popular and pleasantly-given natural history."—*Spectator.*

Jennett Cragg, the Quakeress. A Story of the Plague. By Maria Wright, author of "The Happy Village;" "The Forge on the Heath," &c. Illustrated. Crown 8vo.

Savonarola, the Florentine Martyr. A Reformer before the Reformation. By Elizabeth Warren. With Illustrations. Second

Two Shillings.

Ronald Clayton's Mistakes, and How he Mended Them. By Miss M. A. Paull. Crown 8vo., cloth, gilt.

Lyndon, the Outcast. By Mrs. Clara L. Balfour. Crown 8vo., cloth, gilt.

Illustrated Songs and Hymns for the Little Ones. Compiled by T. B. S. Crown 8vo., cloth.

My Text Roll. Containing 31 large Engraved Texts in Handsome Borders, for hanging on the Walls of Rooms. With Illuminated cover.

A More Excellent Way; and other Stories of the Women's Temperance Crusade in America. By M. E. Winslow. With eight full-page Engravings. Cloth.

The Household Angel in Disguise. By Mrs. M. Leslie. With illustrations. Cloth.

Three People. By Pansy. A Story of the Temperance Crusade in America. Cloth.

Father Rutland; or, the Ban of St. Peter. A Story of the Marian Persecution. By F. I. Tylcoat. Frontispiece. Post 8vo., cloth.

The Hunchback of Carrigmore; An Irish Tale. By J. F. Scott. With Frontispiece. Post 8vo., cloth.

May Lester; or, The Fruits of Self-denial. By Mrs. John Brett, author of "The Belton's Christmas Pudding," &c. Illustrations. Imp. 16mo., cloth, gilt.

Earth's Diamonds; or, Coal, its Formation and value. By Henry H. Bourn, author of "Black Diamonds," etc., with Engravings, cloth, lettered.

"The dangers and difficulties of those who labour underground are very graphically described."—*Rock*.

Till the Goal be Reached. A Temperance Tale. By J. McL. Imperial 16mo., with Engravings, cloth, lettered.

His Charge; or, Corner-Crag Chase. A Temperance Tale. By Maggie Fearn, author of "The Pledged Eleven." Imperial 16mo., cloth, lettered. With Six Engravings.

One Shilling and Sixpence.

Down in the Valley. A Tale. By Lady Hope, Author of

One Shilling and Sixpence—*Continued.*

Jemmy Lawson; The Story of a Village Lad. By E. C. Kenyon, author of "Jack's Heroism," etc. Crown 8vo., cloth extra. Illustrated.

T. B. Smithies, Editor of "The British Workman." A memoir. By G. Stringer Rowe. With Portrait. Crown 8vo., cloth. (Roan gilt, 3s.)

Lory Bell. A Story about Trust in God. By Kate Wood, author of "A Waif of the Sea," &c. Illustrations. Crown 8vo., cloth, gilt.

Brands Plucked from the Burning, and how they were Saved. By the Rev. J. H. Wilson, D.D. Illustrated. New and revised edition. Cloth.

Jessie Macdonald: or, Maidens Beware! By G. S. Williams, author of "Queen Elfrida of the Olden Time." Crown 8vo., cloth, gilt.

Jack's Heroism. A Story of Schoolboy Life. By Edith C. Kenyon. With many Illustrations. Cloth.

Our duty to Animals. By Mrs. C. Bray, author of "Physiology for Schools," &c. Intended to teach the young kindness to animals. Cloth. (*School Edition*, 1/3.)

Richard Slade. A Story for Young and Old. By Charles Ernest. Crown 8vo., cloth, gilt.

Light and Rest; or, The Confessions of a Soul Seeking and Finding. A book for thoughtful inquirers.

"A most helpful book to every anxious inquirer after soul-rest."—*Derbyshire Courier.*

Music for the Nursery. Revised by Philip Phillips, the "Singing Pilgrim." A collection of fifty of the Sweet Pieces for the "Little Ones" that appeared in the "Infant's magazine," &c. Handsomely bound in cloth.

Rag and Tag. A Plea for the Waifs and Strays of Old England. By Mrs. E. J. Whittaker. With ten full-page Engravings. Cloth.

Rills from the Fountain of Life. By the Rev. Dr. Newton. With Illustrations. Cloth.

Sparks from the Anvil. By Elihu Burritt. Cloth.

Stories for Sunday. By Rev. Theron Brown. With numerous illustrations. Cloth.

One Shilling and Sixpence—Continued.

Hours with Girls. By Mrs. Margaret E. Sangster, author of "May Stanhope and Her Friends," "Splendid Times," &c. With full-page Illustrations. Cloth.

Illustrated Sabbath Facts; or, God's weekly gift to the Weary. Reprinted from the "British Workman." With illustrations. 1st and 2nd series. Cloth.

Illustrated Temperance Anecdotes; or, Facts and Figures for the Platform and the People. Compiled by the Editor of the "British Workman." 1st and 2nd series. Cloth.

Ellerslie House. A book for boys. By Emma Leslie. With eight full-page Engravings. Cloth.

The Four Pillars of Temperance. By the author of "Buy your own Cherries." Cloth.

Good Servants, Good Wives, and Happy Homes. By the Rev. T. H. Walker. Cloth.

The Great Pilot and His Lessons. By the author of "The Giants, and how to fight them." With numerous Illustrations. Cloth.

Hilda; or Life's Discipline. By Edith C. Kenyon. With numerous Illustrations. Cloth.

Anecdotes of Aborigines; Historical and Missionary. With several Illustrations. Cloth.

Bible Wonders. By the Rev. Dr. Newton. With numerous illustrations. Cloth.

Bible Jewels. By the Rev. Dr. Newton. With numerous Illustrations. Cloth.

The Brewer's Son. By the late Mrs. Ellis, author of "The Women of England," "Daughters of England," &c. With several Illustrations. Cloth.

The Dairyman's Daughter. By the Rev. Legh Richmond, M.A. Cloth.

Kitty King. A Book for the Nursery. With full-page Engravings. Cloth.

The Little Woodman and his Dog Cæsar. By Mrs. Sherwood. Illustrations. Cloth.

Manchester House. A Tale of Two Apprentices. By J.

One Shilling and Sixpence—Continued.

Satisfied. By Mrs. Trowbridge. Cloth.

Household Angel in Disguise. By M. Leslie. Paper Boards. 8vo. (Cloth, 2s.)

Martha the Merry; or, as One Door Shuts another Opens. A book for Girls. By Mrs. Jerome Mercier. Second edition. With Engravings. Crown 8vo., cloth.
"A pleasing story, and well told."—*Weekly Review.*

Facts to Impress, Fancies to Delight. A book for young people. By Frederic T. Gammon. Crown 8vo. Many Illustrations. Cloth.
"Presented in a style that must prove eminently attractive to the young."—*Christian Leader.*

The Canal Boy who became President. By the same author. Sixth edition. Twentieth Thousand. Crown 8vo. Illustrated. Cloth.
"A handsome volume, the contents of which are really golden."—*Norwich Argus.*

The Little Bugler. A Tale of the American Civil War. By George Monroe Royce. With Engravings. Cloth, lettered.
"It is a book which boys will devour with great avidity; and it ought to command a large circle of readers."—*Commonwealth.*

Burton Brothers. A Temperance Tale. Founded on Fact. By Laura L. Pratt. Crown 8vo., cloth.

The Blue Ribbon Text Book. (A handsome and valuable present to persons signing the pledge) with spaces for autographs, and Portrait of Mr. Noble.

The Gospel Temperance Text Book. Cloth lettered.

Chapters in Irish History. By W. B. Kirkpatrick, D.D., Second edition. Crown 8vo., cloth.

Life Truths. By the Rev. J. Denham Smith. 16mo., cloth. (Paper, fourteenth thousand, 6d.)

Life in Christ. By the same author. 16mo., cloth.

Things you ought to Know about Yourself; or, Sketches of Human Physiology. By R. T. Kaufmann. With Illustrations. Crown 8vo., cloth.
"A popular hand-book on human physiology."—*Fountain.*

Great Pyramid: Its History and Teachings. With Diagram. By T. Septimus Marks. Second edition. Limp. (Cloth, 2s.)

One Shilling.

Sir Moses Montefiore. The Story of his Life. By James Weston, Author of "Joseph Livesey," etc. With Portrait and Illustrations. Crown 8vo., cloth extra.

Joseph Livesey. The Story of his Life, 1794—1884. By James Weston. With Portraits. Crown 8vo., cloth extra.

John Harris, the Cornish Poet. The Story of his Life. By his son, J. Howard Harris. With Portrait. Crown 8vo., cloth extra.

Shaftesbury: His Life and Work. By G. Holden Pike, author of "The Romance of the Streets," etc. With Portrait and Illustrations. Crown 8vo., cloth extra.

John Wicliffe; or, the Morning Star of the Reformation. By David J. Deane, author of "Martin Luther." Many Illustrations. Crown 8vo., cloth extra.

Martin Luther, the Reformer. Written in a Popular Style for the Young. Many Illustrations. Crown 8vo., cloth.

Lilies; or Letters to School Girls. By well-known Writers. Royal 16mo., cloth extra, 1s.

Nan's Story; or The Life and Work of a City Arab. By L. Sharp. Crown 8vo., cloth extra. Illustrated.

Bible Pictures and Stories. By James Weston, author of "Dick's Holidays," etc. With forty-six beautiful full-page Illustrations by W. J. Webb, Sir John Gilbert, and others. Fcap. 4to. Illustrated Boards.

Pretty Pictures for our Little Ones, with Descriptive Stories by James Weston, author of "Dick's Holidays," etc. With forty-six beautiful Illustrations by Robert Barnes and others. Fcap. 4to. Illustrated Boards.

Cloister and Closet. A Plea for Private Meditation. By Rev. C. E. Stone. Demy 16mo., cloth extra.

Stories and Illustrations of the Ten Commandments. With Illustrations. Cloth.

Toil and Trust; or, Life of Patty, the Workhouse Girl. By Mrs. Balfour. Illustrations. Cloth.

Truth frae 'mang the Heather; or, Is the Bible True; By William M'Caw, Shepherd. With Portrait. Cloth.

Wanderings of a Bible, and My Mother's Bible. With Illustrations. Cloth.

One Shilling—Continued.

Widow Green and her Three Nieces. By Mrs. Ellis. With Illustrations. Cloth.

Willie Heath and the House Rent. By William Leask, D.D. Cloth.

Divine and Moral Songs. By Dr. Watts. With illustrations. Cloth.

Frank Spencer's Rule of Life. By J. W. Kirton, author of "Buy your own Cherries." With Illustrations. Cloth.

Frying-Pan Alley. By Mrs. C. A. West. With illustrations by R. Barnes. Cloth.

The Giants and How to Fight Them. By the Rev. Dr. Newton. Illustrations. Cloth.

The Governess; or, The Missing Pencil Case. Cloth.

"Have we any Word of God?" By the author of "Is the Bible True?" With Illustrations. Cloth.

How Paul's Penny became a Pound. By Mrs. Bowen, author of "Dick and His Donkey." With Illustrations. Cloth.

How Peter's Pound became a Penny. By the author of "Jack the Conqueror," &c. With Illustrations. Cloth.

Jenny's Geranium; or, the Prize Flower of a London Court. With Illustrations. Cloth.

The Battlefield. A Tale of the East-end of London. By the author of "Frying-pan Alley." With Illustrations. Cloth.

Bible Pattern of a Good Woman. By Mrs. Balfour. Cloth.

Birdie and Her Dog, and other Stories of Canine Sagacity. By Miss Phillips. With Illustrations. Cloth.

"Buster" and "Baby Jim." By the author of "Blue Flag," &c. With four illustrations by R. Barnes. Cloth

Cared for; or, the Orphan Wanderers. By Mrs. C. E. Bowen, author of "Dick and His Donkey," &c. With illustrations. Cloth.

One Shilling—Continued.

Plea for Mercy to Animals. By Dr. Macaulay, Editor of "The Leisure Hour." With illustrations. Cheap Edition. Cloth.

Prince Consort, The Late. Reminiscences of his Life and Character. By the Rev. J. H. Wilson. With numerous illustrations. Cloth.

Rosa; or, The Two Castles. By Miss Bradburn. With eight full-page Engravings. Cloth.

The Water Waifs. By Emma Leslie. With seven full-page Engravings. Cloth.

Only a Little Fault. By Emma Leslie. With seven full-page Engravings. Cloth.

God's Arithmetic; (intended chiefly for the Young Members of the Family). By Mrs. F. West. With five full-page Engravings. Cloth.

A Mother's Stories for her Children. By the late Mrs. Carus Wilson. Cloth.

Mind Whom You Marry; or, The Gardener's Daughter. By the Rev. C. G. Rowe. Cloth.

No Gains without Pains. A True Story. By H. C. Knight. Cloth.

Moderate Drinking. Containing the speeches on the above subject by Sir H. Thompson, F.R C.S.; Dr. B. W. Richardson, F.R.S.; Rev. Canon Farrar, D.D., F.R.S.; Sir Edward Baines; Admiral Sir James Sullivan, K.C.B.; and Rev. H. Sinclair Paterson, M.D. With Portraits of the above speakers. Cloth. (Without Portraits, and first three speeches only, paper cover, 4d.)

Our Ten Weeks' Strike. By G. E. Sargent, author of "The Story of a Pocket Bible." With Illustrations. Cloth.

Poor Blossom. The Story of a Horse. By E.H.B. With many Illustrations. Cloth.

"Puffing Billy" and the Prize "Rocket"; or, The Story of the Stephensons and our Railways. By Mrs. H. C. Knight. Illustrations. Cloth.

A Mother's Lessons on the Lord's Prayer. By the late Mrs. C. L. Balfour. With many Illustrations. Cloth.

One Shilling—Continued.

John Oriel's Start in Life. By Mary Howitt. With many Illustrations. Cloth.

Kindness to Animals. By Charlotte Elizabeth. With numerous Illustrations. Cloth.

Cheering Words for Weary and Troubled Believers. By Rev. Alfred Tyler. Second Edition, 16mo., cloth.

"It will be as a rivulet of comfort to many a pilgrim in the wilderness of this world."—*Derbyshire Courier.*

The "Fear-Nots" of Scripture; or, Apples of Gold in Pictures of Silver. By Miss Catherine M Meade. 16mo., cloth.

"A cheerful tone pervades the book, and it will tend greatly to scatter doubts and fears, and in their place produce hope and assurance."—*Derbyshire Courier.*

I Know; or, the Verities of the Bible. By Mrs. Peploe, authoress of "Naomi," &c. Second thousand. 16mo. cloth.

"A healthful book for doubters and fearers, containing things important to be known, set out in plain and forcible language."—*The Christian.*

Polished Corner Stones; or, Letters to School Girls. By Popular writers. Royal 16mo., cloth.

Women of the Bible. (Old Testament.) By Etty Woosnam. Third edition. Royal 16mo., cloth.

Women of the Bible. (New Testament.) By Etty Woosnam. Royal 16mo., cloth.

Industrial Homes and their Management; for the Labouring Classes. By H. L. Hamilton. Foolscap 8vo., cloth.

Lectures on Bible Difficulties. By Rev. G. D. Copeland, B.D., Vicar of St. Stephen's, Walworth. Second edition. Paper. (Limp cloth, 1s. 6d.)

"Marvellously refreshing to the man of meditation."—*South London Observer.*

The Happiness of Full Consecration. Being brief memorials of Emmeline Duncan. Second edition. Cloth.

"An instructive and edifying record of Christian experience, showing that whole-heartedness brings power with both God and man."—*The Christian.*

The Sabbath made for Man. Being the essay awarded an Extra Prize by the Adjudicators of the Lord's Day Observance Society. By Rev. G. A. Jacob, D.D. Crown 8vo., paper. (Cloth,

One Shilling—Continued.

The Holy Life. A Book for Christians Seeking the Rest of Faith. By the Rev. Evan H. Hopkins. Cheaper edition. Cloth.

Ninepence.

The Adventures of "Wouldn't-say-Wee." By Nasr-ed-Din Sparrow, R.A. Edited by F. I. Tylcoat. With Illustrations. Royal 16mo, cloth.

"One of the sweetest pleas on behalf of birds, that ever it was our pleasure to read"—*Sword and Trowel.*

Luther: his Life and Work. Written in a popular style for the Young. Many Illustrations. Crown 8vo. (Cloth 1s.)

James Sullivan; or, Ready for the Turn of the Tide. By Grace Stebbing, author of "Walter Benn," &c. Fcap. 8vo., cloth.

Grandpapa's Missionary Stories of Ancient and Modern Times. For the Young. By W. Campbell, late of Bangalore. With Illustrations. Fcap. 8vo., cloth.

Ben Owen; a Lancashire Story. By Jennie Perrett. Second edition. With Engravings. Fcap. 8vo., cloth.

Into the Light. By the same author. Fcap. 8vo., cloth.

A Railway Line to Fortune; or, the Power of a Good Name. By the author of "Tom Knight." Frontispiece. Small 8vo., cloth.

"Vic": the Autobiography of a Pomeranian Dog. By Alfred C. Fryer, Ph.D., M.A. Cloth.

The Adventures of Gustavus Wasa; or, the Dawning of Light in Sweden. By L. S. Griffith. With Illustrations. Royal 16mo., cloth.

"Boys will delight in a book like this, with its graphic sketches of the eventful career of the greatest of Swedish kings."—*Primitive Methodist.*

Grace Thornton; or, Living for Others. A Tale. By F. C. G. With Illustrations. Royal 16mo., cloth.

"Intended to stimulate moral and religious impulses."—*Literary World.*

Patsy; or, One of His Little Ones. With Engravings. Royal 16mo., cloth.

A pleasing story of an Orphan Boy and his Dog "Beauty."

Lightning Source UK Ltd.
Milton Keynes UK
UKOW04f0609300517
302287UK00009B/618/P